CRIES TO MOTHER

NATURE

ISBN (eBook/Kindle): 979-8-90379-920-6

ISBN (Paperback): 979-8-90379-921-3

ISBN (Hardcover): 979-8-90379-922-0

Library Of Congress Catalog Card Number: Applied

Published in the United States of America by Lynx Publishers.

CRIES TO MOTHER

NATURE

MOTHER EARTH PLEADS FOR HELP

CINDY FREBE

PROLOGUE

Mother Nature and Mother Earth, joined by cosmic forces, continue the fight against destruction and despair. Their story is one of sorrow, resilience, and ultimately, hope. They call upon all. Humans, animals, children, and advocates must stand together and protect the planet to restore harmony. The urgency is clear, the belief in goodness and unity remains steadfast. Only through collective effort and the courage to confront evil can the world be healed and its natural wonders preserved for generations to come.

Cindy Frebe

THE CRY OF MOTHER EARTH

Narrated by Cindy Frebe

In a tranquil meadow nestled deep within an ancient forest, Mother Nature descends from her celestial home on Venus to visit Mother Earth. Their conversation unfolds amidst towering trees and the gentle stirrings of spring, revealing the burdens Mother Earth carries and the interconnectedness of all living things.

Resting upon a boulder surrounded by her lovely animals of all kinds, and hints of spring peeking through the winter carpet. She brushes her hand across the rock and softly speaks.

*Hello Mother Earth, I've come down
to see how you're feeling today.*

With a sigh and in a voice not nearly as strong as she used to be, Mother Earth replies, "Hello, my friend, it is so good to see you. I am feeling so tired lately. I've usually been able to restore myself after the effects the humans have on my resources, but now, well, they have come at me from within by injecting poisons deep into my veins." Sighing, she continues, "It's making me sick, and I am getting pressure in odd areas. I cannot help these earthquakes. It's my only way to release, and I am having trouble not just letting all this gas they want out myself and be done with it!"

Frowning, Mother Nature looked out across the beautiful landscape, which was her friend, and could hear the sadness in her voice.

"Hold steady, my friend," she softly says, "I still have faith in the human souls here. I believe they are finding out just how fragile you are becoming with some of the practices being used. I see them working hard to save you, but they are fighting a tough fight and need much more help across the lands. I see the new generation of children is set to protect you, and they are coming out in force. It makes me so proud to watch them succeed, but I fear you need much more help than they can provide you. We need more humans to assist them in achieving their goal."

With a chuckle that seemed to vibrate the ground, Mother Earth states, "Well, you have been busy showing off your power in these storms, such great force and in areas that rarely see your power. Do you think it will make a difference?"

Now looking somewhat fierce and concerned, Mother Nature's tone becomes serious. "That's why I am here, my friend. My intent is not to be so severe, but these changes in your core temperature are affecting the weather seasons, and I am beginning to worry about the power they are producing. The animals of the lands are crying out due to the loss of shelters and food, and I am losing many of them every day."

"I need help," she continues, "and the humans are the only ones who can correct this. I cannot seem to get my concerns to them to make them understand what will happen if they don't."

Mother Earth's smile reflects in the morning sunrise. "I have been seeing a change in the humans here myself. I can feel the concern of so many, and they are starting to make a change, but they are themselves fighting a tough battle to save me, knowing I need that so much as you do, my friend. I am here to provide shelter, food, water, and so much more, including your animals, which are in serious need."

"I cannot grow my trees any faster, and they are used for more than just shelters for people. They are used to clean the air for instance. They are a multisource resource," she chuckles.

"The humans are taking down the ones I've done my best to protect, some of the most important, and that's something I cannot fix in a timely manner."

Lowering her head in sadness, Mother Nature softly says, "I hear the cries of the animals, the loss of habitat and food; not to mention the new poisons used to kill anything on contact!"

She lifts her head as the anger begins to show. "Why must they kill everything? I don't understand," shaking her head and beginning to pace about.

"I feel it, you know! All of it!"

"Whoa now, calm yourself, or another Nor'easter is going to form," Mother Earth chuckles, attempting to soothe the anger in her friend.

Mother Nature, in all seriousness, says, "Well, I am not going to stop these storms until humans stop harming you! This madness of destroying your inner core with poisonous injection deep in the depths and the horrendous bomb testing not only in the ground but in your waters. My goodness, I'm running out of solutions. I need the human souls to simply assist me: do they not see that?"

"I feel so repetitive, I am always asking the same questions and receiving the same answers, yet it is never enough to resolve the problems. We need more."

"I can feel the love from the humans," Mother Earth reassures.

"They are coming together more now than I have seen before, and it's giving me hope and strength. You see them too, I know, caring for your animals, my forests and waters with complete heart and soul. Searching and using their skills together to find solutions to protect me. They give me hope, that's for sure. Cleaning up my waters is showing big changes for the chain of life. I am so grateful."

Smiling softly, Mother Nature responds, "You're right, my friend. I see this new generation working hard to correct all the hardships and destruction that have been inflicted on you for far too long. With the world of humans working together, we can begin to help heal and rebuild the wounds inflicted on you. I would be nothing without you, Mother Earth. I am the caretaker of living things, and that includes you."

"Aw, my dear, your passion is contagious, but the fact is, without each other, there is nothing at all. That is what humans do not completely understand."

"So true. It has been wonderful visiting with you, my friend, but I must be going. I will be back soon." Mother Nature prepares to leave. "Lots of work to get to"

"Your visits are my favorite times,"

Mother Earth replies, "I will help you any way I can."

"Stay strong, I am off to see conditions for myself, lots to be done."

Mother Nature ascends into the clouds in the sky with hope in her heart for the future of Mother Earth and determination to call together all she can in the hopes of saving the precious animals and humans sharing the beautiful world on Earth.

Back in her home, she begins to pace back and forth on the balcony of her home. She is surrounded by some of her most beautiful animals, most of which have become extinct on Earth due to the environmental damage and excessive hunting caused by humans for years, so much is being wasted to better their own lives. On a giant redwood tree in her forest nearby, she is enjoying the sounds of the Imperial woodpecker as they introduce a new addition to their family. As the species numbers decreased, Mother Nature will save them from Earth to either return them later or allow them the habitat of her beloved home, hidden under the clouds of Venus.

"How am I going to stop this madness?" she asks the animals. "How can we save your descendants and allow the new generations to prevail?"

The animals sang out in unison, "The children, Ma'am."

"What do you mean, the children?" she asks as the hum of agreement throughout the land turned into the most beautiful chorus.

"The children are our only chance of survival," Dodi, the Dodo bird, speaks up next to her.

"Hello Dodi," she smiles at him, "how to do it, is the hard part."

"What about the listeners? Those on earth that connect with the animals have that special ability to communicate without even knowing it. It is their gift, and we need to call upon them now."

Mother laughs softly, "The listeners," you call them?"

"Yes, we do. Just like Jane Goodall, for example. She has already been starting to get the children involved, and it is working really well." Dodi begins to flap his wings with excitement.

"Hmmm, I'll have to really think about that, Dodi. Jane's accomplishments with conservation and saving my beloved animals are unique, and I need so many more like her right now. You do make a good point about the younger ones still unsure of the powers they have."

"I have a youngster in mind that we have been watching for a long time, you remember little Synnia, the little girl that the forest animals called you about. She was so small and alone, and the animals watched over her."

"Oh yes! She has very strong powers without even knowing it, and it may be time to contact her and the others, too. Thank you, Dodi, for some great advice. You leave me with a lot to think about and plan."

There were so many souls with the power to change; Mother Nature may need to reach out to the Almighty for assistance in her plan. Surely the need for help is good enough to awaking the silent helpers on Earth to come forth and save Earth.

THE WHALES ARE CRYING

One morning on her balcony at her home amongst the clouds, she begins to hear the saddest calls from her Northwest pod of Orca whales.

"I must go and find out what is going on down there that is making the whales cry out so loud." She begins to descend into the beautiful waters of the Pacific Northwest, where the sound and waterways are filled with Salmon for the whales to eat. As she gets closer, the sight before her is the saddest thing she has ever seen. One of her beloved mother whales has finally had an addition to her family pod, and what should have been such a joyous occasion quickly changed as the young whale had not survived. The mother is so distraught that she is now carrying it across her nose and refusing to let it go. Pain and frustration is evident in her eyes.

"Mother whale," she says softly. In her moment of sadness the mother whale looks up to her.

"The salmon are too few to find," she cried, "the humans are poisoning the waters, and they are using sounds and pressures in the depths that are killing us. All of our efforts to get help are ignored. I am showing my dead baby to all in the hopes they understand and help us. I fear the humans cannot help us. I have carried my child up and down this coastline, and yet they do not understand."

Mother Nature gently speaks, "My beautiful creature, I see and hear your cries. They are not in vain! I see many of our human friends standing up against the cruel and indifferent evils that are set on destruction."

"Hold steady, my child. I am aware of the crisis of so many, and solutions are being decided. Your child is with my beloved animals, which have crossed to what is to come and will be cared for by generations of your kind there. Stay strong." On a rock near the shore of the ocean, Mother Nature sits gently touching her beautiful whale, sharing a moment of love and silence.

Sometime later, she ascends again into the skies to her beloved home, ready to activate the conversations needed to protect the animals upon her friend Mother Earth. So much to do.

Awakening in the next Earth morning, there is an immense amount of chatter coming from Mother Earth.

"My goodness," she says, "what is going on now? I must speak to Mother Earth right away. There is so much turmoil."

As she descends to her favorite location in the Amazon rainforest, she speaks to Mother Earth. As she waits, she glances around and is struck by the destruction to the rainforest since her last visit.

"What is this!" She cries, The forest is destroyed, and by the greed of humans themselves. Do they not know what they have done? Deep cuts in the crust of the earth, removing and disturbing ancient forests in the most sacred of locations. Protected by some of her most lethal animals to protect her from the humans, and hidden beneath the vegetation, lying dormant are the viruses that, if disturbed, can wreak havoc on the earth and its inhabitants.

"Mother Earth," she calls out, "are you ok?"

Sighing, Mother Earth softly speaks out, "No, I am afraid I am not. I am being destroyed from all sides, and I cannot stop it. There is a new virus out now, and mankind is close to destruction; it is all I can do to protect myself from the despicable treatment of myself, the land, and the animals that protect me."

Mother Nature listens and states, "It is very fast spreading, I see. There is a lot of chatter from all around. The humans seem to turn on themselves in a time of need instead of working together. I notice it is the elderly and sick who are taken ill so fast, I suggest, Mother Earth, that we do our best to direct this crisis to those destructive humans who are set on destroying you Yes she says in frustration, It seems to me we may be able to remove some evil souls as a last resort to protect ourselves and the dedicated souls protecting you and me. I do not normally feel this type of urgency, but this virus should not be awake."

"I did not wake up this virus; mankind did. Mother Nature, in her frustration, speaks out. But I do agree that taking an extra step of removing the cruel first is something you and I can work on together. I am not sure the Almighty would allow us to, we may need to consult first. But, maybe we can use some of your animal armies to direct our powers towards the evil set to destroy us and the goodness in our world."

"I agree, Mother Nature. Let's begin our plans to transition now and move this towards evil thinkers and doers."

"Brilliant! Mother Earth, I agree and have already been shifting the spread myself, but of course, I cannot do it without you or cosmic approval to interfere. I will have this discussion, but meanwhile, remember that we are one, my friend, and I cannot exist without you, and you without me. I feel a shift coming, and we must prepare for it. I will meet up with you again soon. Take care of yourself."

Alone in her home, Mother Nature ponders. It is so quiet, the world itself is now in quarantine, and an invisible and deadly virus has been awoken to spread death and fear all upon the Earth.

Mother Nature, with much determination and a fierce protectiveness for her animals and Earth, gazes below to the utterly deafening sound of sadness. Quietly, she descends to her bench for a moment with her friend.

"How are you, my friend?" she says.

"The fear and sadness in my world are at levels I haven't felt for so long."

"I know, but please continue to hold steady. I'm working with my children all over, far and wide. We will fight this influx of evil and destruction using the same weapon they have sent to the innocent."

"Mess with me, I say!! That is something they are not worried about, which is alarming."

"It's been a while. How are you feeling, Mother Earth?"

"Well, the virus has slowed down the injections into my core, which has given me time for countermeasures to protect myself. I thank you for that. The humans are scared, and I wish those working so hard knew just how much they were already doing to protect me was helping me."

"Did you hear the singing?" she says with a smile, "such a beautiful sound, and we need so much more. It has a healing effect."

Mother Earth sighs softly and says, "But this evil is so strong this time. Do you have enough strength to protect me, my friend?"

"I've got you," Mother Nature assures. "This is not going to be easy for sure, but it will root out the evil that has been festering in this world and gotten powerful enough to destroy itself and the Universe. So please believe me, we will be ok. I have entrusted my animals with the direct instructions to seek out and protect the virus so that it will not be altered by humans. And I promise to you, Mother Earth, the parties that may have altered this virus to harm humans as they try to advance the destruction of our world will not succeed. Not this time or any other."

"With all my powers, Almightys, the Cosmos and Earths, I hereby direct the animal's society to seek out evil and deflect to protect our future. All of the evil, self-centered souls that currently walk across your land will now and forever suffer. Greed will be the candy of sorts for a virus. The greedier you are, the sicker you will be. Lies will increase symptoms, and selfishness shall kill you. We give our power of protection to our human souls across the world, doing all we can to help each other. We offer you our power of protection to use for yourselves, your families, and those you fight so hard to save."

"Please know that the heavens are in full-service mode, but no matter what, we will come together and be in a better place. We know the evil was spreading, but our guard was not up enough to see just how fast it was changing. But goodness, kindness, and love are flowing now all over the world. We see it, we feel it, we are fighting with you. We must all work together to achieve true freedom from evil. I myself am frustrated and frantic in my thoughts. Let us take a moment to rest and focus. I shall be back soon."

A beautiful morning has approached, and Mother Earth is feeling so very different this morning. "Hmmm," she says, "my core has not felt such rest in a long time. It should not take long, and I may be able to restore the destruction caused to me. The humans are singing, they are scared, and I want so badly to help them. But this virus has caused the world to stop, and the effects are positive for me. I must tell Mother Nature about my findings; she should be here soon."

At that, a twinkle in the sky and in a beautiful halo of light, Mother Nature came into her private meadow where she sits with Mother Earth.

With a sigh, Mother Nature speaks softly to Mother Earth, "Hello, my friend, you are looking well today."

Mother Earth shares her findings of how the shutdown upon her is working, but it won't last long enough for full repair.

"That is wonderful news, my friend. However, you are correct that there will not be enough time. The evil is so strong, the people are trying so hard, yet they are blocked by their own kind. I do not understand this. This is not right, and my anger is rising. Mother Earth, we must address this more ourselves than only helping the good souls; we must speak with the almighty on how we may proceed, and if we can intervene for them. Meanwhile, I am calling on my animal kingdoms far and wide all around the world; the humans need help from some of their own, and we will fight with them in our quest to rid you of these evil, destructive souls set to annihilate our world. THIS WILL NOT HAPPEN."

Mother Earth interrupts gently, "Ah, my friend. I am with you all the way, but I agree the anguish coming from my core is downright painful. The almighty and our angels above are so very busy with the outcry from here. I have some ideas for our fight for life. Let us add that the more they lie and cheat, the stronger my storms will be. We can interrupt their plans at least and get us more time for the deserving humans to prevail. I will shake them off this planet until each and every one of them is gone."

That is what this Mother Earth wants to do, she says with mischief in her tone. The evil is strong, but love, compassion, and camaraderie will ALWAYS have more power than evil. I believe we should step up our help.

"Mother Earth! That's it."

"Oh, really, what part Mother Nature?"

"We need to expand the inner powers of our human partners." Mother Nature's mind begins to form a plan.

"With all the powers in myself, Mother Earth and our Almighty's I spread to mankind the increase of inner power, kindness, and strength to each and every soul that calls upon us for assistance. I direct all my animals, all shapes and sizes, to descend around the earth and help us support the humans that need our help and weed out the destructive humans that have no purpose on earth other than destruction, greed, and meanness. I direct my powers to the viruses to lessen in deserving souls and hit with a vengeance on the evil souls spread around the world. I demand with all my powers granted to me the protection of the untainted souls. That evil and greed are now the food of choice for incurable diseases, viruses, and cancers. With all my might, I send this order throughout the lands. Hear me now and heed my words. We are sending evil backwards. I give strength, courage, and knowledge to all as a shield to fight this fight. We will combat and win, we will go on, we will be better."

The determination and power in Mother Nature's words stirred up the powerful Elements that Mother Earth has for defense. The powers that be have been instructed, and to work they will go. Mother Earth will increase earthquakes, tornadoes, hurricanes, floods, sweltering heats, freezing colds, missing seasons needed for their food, and more to awaken the people around the world that this is no longer acceptable.

Mother Earth chuckles softly, "Oh, the strength you have, my friend. It is spectacular to see and fills me with hope. I thank you so much, I have much more to do. The evils are doing things...wicked things, while humans are fighting to survive. I will expose all they do; they cannot hide from me. I plan to shake them, flood them, burn them, or freeze them. Whatever it takes, we shall do. Your power and mine combined, with our human friends, will wipe out this virus that has been spread throughout the land. I do hope the humans have the strength to stand with us. The goodness walking my lands is in dire need of more to stand with them. I wish they understood this is all for them, but we cannot do it all ourselves."

Mother Nature replies, " We have seen this before, my old friend. Many times, we have watched the good light fade as the darkness of greed and evil prevailed. We did not involve ourselves, but this time is very different. This time, the darkness is strong, and we must all combat it. We have much to do, my friend. I will come back soon, but meanwhile, let's get busy and rock this world, Mother Earth."

Another Earth morning, and Mother Nature gazes down upon the Earth. In a whisper to the circle of life, she says, "Stand strong and stand together, my friends. For I am working with our mother Earth, the Sun, and the Moon, the Cosmos, along with our Great Almighty and the team of angels that spread their wings around mother Earth, we are increasing the love, strength, courage, and confidence the people seek. They need hope, and we shall send it."

Sighing, she says softly, "Oh, my soul is heavy with the blanket of sadness. Hold steady, everyone. I am so proud of all the love throughout the lands; it is what increases my strength, which will help us all." Her voice drifts throughout the cosmos, across the galaxies, and upon the lands of Earth.

Many Earth days have passed, and the virus is rapidly changing as directed by Mother Nature, and dedicated humans are working to protect the humans, and it is working. The world is coming together as one. Yet there is still the exception of the single-minded, selfish individuals who seem to lack any moral response to the catastrophe spreading across the world.

"Hmmmm," Mother Nature sits quietly, gazing towards Earth, and sees that the turmoil is increasing rapidly. She sighs and is encouraged by the amount of kindness, love, and compassion that is pulsing in the Earth. Thinking to herself, 'How is there so much evil power still. It seems to be growing and not shrinking. This whole thing should not have happened. The abuse of Mother Earth and my beautiful animals has reached a level of destruction that is just too much to recover from and is detrimental to our entire universe. Where is this power of hate and cruelty coming from?'

As she sits with her thoughts, a beautiful, bright light begins to form, coming closer to her as she sits upon her balcony. "Ahh," she says, "I have company."

Mother Nature looks across at the glorious glow and, feeling a sense of calm again, she sighs and speaks, "Hello, my friend. It is so good to see you. Please join me here. I have an important situation on Earth I need to discuss and it is becoming quite worrisome, as she describes her conversations she continues, Mother Earth and I do understand and agree that this is meant to be as our last resort to stop such horrid destruction and cruelty towards humans, animals, and the Earth. But the evil has spread so far and so fast that good souls are dying, and we can feel it." Mother Nature stops for a moment. The presence of the Almighty himself in her home spoke volumes to her. She turned and smiled.

"I'm sorry, I did not even give you a proper hello, welcome, or how are you doing. My apologies to you."

"Ahh, Mother Nature. I needed to come to you myself, for my kingdom is quite busy with this increase of evil, hate, and destruction. It has filled the heavens, and we feel yours and Mother Earth's sorrows."

"I am so very proud of you all. This is a strong decision for me, but one in which I could root out the evil to be fought by the humans themselves. I feel the love, and it envelopes me with light, reminding me that together as one, the humans are invincible. I see they are standing strong. But Mother Nature, the amount of hate, disconnect, and selfishness of all parts of evil are embedded much deeper than any of us knew. So, I have this new pandemic to keep them in the homes. I like to think I've grounded them to their homes for time to ponder why they're on earth and what they really should be doing. Old evil Luce has been much busier than I thought, although I was saddened at just how easy it was for humans to turn or be turned again."

Mother Nature smiles, "Grounded them." Laughing, she says, "what a great way to put it. It has been so uplifting to see the goodness, kindness, and compassion. But the suffering is growing. I've been working with Mother Earth."

She chuckles, "She'll like the grounding part. She said she hasn't felt this good in thousands of years. Her air is cleaner, water is cleaner, and they are not injecting poison into her. But she has the elements giving her some assistance in the cleanout. The storms are strong and fierce, but I needed to help restore some strength to her."

"We're succeeding. I know. But it will take us all working together to make it through. Luce's evil is so much stronger than before. We need to extend extra protection for humans. I would like your help in discounting the falsehoods that Luce is instilling. He is growing greed and cruelty at an accelerated rate. A reminder of your power is what is needed."

"The humans have a medicine already, I believe Luce's followers have interfered within a virus which removed my ability of control. I am furious about this; it will always be unacceptable to fool with me."

"I have now modified it as best as I can and enlisted the help of Mother Earth and my animals to return it to the originators, who themselves think they are protected from its strength. I cannot remove it, but it will lose its ability to destroy so immediately. I ask that we work together to increase the human spirit, confidence, and knowledge for those fighting for humanity. I seem to say it a lot, yet it is something that needs constant focus. Most importantly, now is the time that we especially focus on the suppression of the evilness consuming the world below us."

Listening intently and with genuine concern, the Almighty says, "Mother Nature, I cannot agree more. I am here today to rejoice with you and Mother Earth that your focus on love and kindness is much stronger than I feared, and that has given me so much more hope for our world."

He chuckles, "Mother Earth has asked to keep the people inside for a bit longer. Says it's the best she has felt in years. But we must remember, it is not our choice; they must choose themselves entirely, but a little helpful guidance from us is now approved by me, and I trust you to know boundaries. This is not something I like to do, but I feel I must."

"Be vigilant, Mother Nature," says the Almighty, deep in thought.

"I am always available and approve of your methods. I thank you for spending time with me today and send my love to Mother Earth. I must get back and assemble my team for what is sure to happen next." With that said, the Almighty shines bright as it lifts off the balcony towards the heavens. Changes on Earth are increasing at an alarming rate, and plans are being constructed.

Later, as Mother Nature gazes out across her land of animals. Most of them are extinct now on Earth. "My children, my beautiful animals, we must do our duty for the humans. Yes, I realize a lot are not worth keeping on our beautiful lands, but so many are. My instructions to you all who are able is to spread out. Find the goodness and protect as best as possible. Our mission is to eliminate the gross amount of evil and destruction that is spreading around this world and is extremely strong. Protect our fellow humans, protect yourselves, and together we will make Mother Earth healthy again."

"Just look at her, already she shines. Her air is cleaner, water is cleaner, and the people are still singing. I feel the love, and it's making me stronger every minute."

As she continues to assemble her thoughts, she is struck by just how much resistance she is seeing in the world. "My goodness, the evil is strong. I do not understand how it turned like it did. The human race has no idea that they will continue to repeat lives until they figure it out. Evil will not succeed in proceeding to our Heavens. That is what Mother Earth is for, but so many are led by someone else's thoughts, wants, and selfish causes." She closes her eyes and summons her greatest powers, spreading her arms out wide and generating an unimaginable beam towards Mother Earth to once again reach her friend and the animal kingdom.

"Hear my words, feel my strength. I am calling on all my animal kingdom, it is with your assistance, and I mean everyone, to protect the goodness left in this world. A virus has been modified against my will, and my anger is real. It has never been a joke to not mess with me, for my patience is strong, but messing with me is Forbidden. I speak out to those who are evil, greedy, and selfish humans. I hereby direct all my kingdom of animals to work together in defeating you with these cruel acts on humanity. I have modified your cheap work to return to sender with no ability to alter it anymore. I say that together with Mother Earth and our Almighty, the time is now. My children, the evil is surrounded by you, and we will not be defeated. I'm offering my powers of protection to the human souls that portray courage, kindness, compassion, and Fight. I spread my protections for you all over the world, but these protections will not protect any forms of evil or negative souls. You must stay strong in convictions, for the evil doers Will Not proceed in Life after death. They will understand that any humans who've altered and destroyed my chain of life, chosen to make decisions that are forbidden on this planet, shall never and will never be allowed on any planet. They will suffer for all eternity."

"I am angry, and my patience is out. These are my words, and with the powers in my control, this is how it shall be!"

With that said, she continues, "Mother Earth is in total agreement; she has already begun to shake off the evil. We hope the humans protect each other as this fight will be complex and include flooding, freezing, heating, and more."

"With my increase in power, I call on all my elements. The Wind, Water, Fire, and Earth shall proceed across the lands and sea and stir up for all to witness."

Her words rang down upon the land, the chain of her kingdom, with pride for their mother, who began planning.

"Knowing amongst the kingdom that it's not going to be easy, but we must succeed. We have had to do this before. Months and weeks go by, and now it's another day on Earth. The humans are in dire straits as the virus continues; time is needed for the unaltered version to take over the current one, which was spreading a quick death throughout the world. The powers which Mother Nature created are working hard, but it is taking time and lives."

"The humans are banding together to fight this fight, but sadly, the great evil has built itself upon our Mother Earth. It is presenting as leaders that are not leaders at all. This spread is out of control, yet the powers that be must find a way to turn it toward its source and allow the destruction of such evil doers to be brutal and final."

From her balcony, Mother Nature again calls out to the kingdom. "With my full powers within me, I have my armies of protection. With this decree, I send to our fighters a cloak of protection for all. She hears her animals across our earth as they stand up and cry out, The time is now, and we will protect those who protect us with all we have."

Mother Nature's words echo across the universe, "for this crisis is affecting all, and it will not stop until this evil mess is corrected. Even though time is different on Earth, it feels extraordinarily long even for her."

As the Earth days pass, Mother Nature is hard at work. She is hearing such happiness from the animals and Mother Earth. In fact, as she gazes out, the air is so much cleaner it's just beautiful. 'I must visit Mother Earth today,' she thinks, 'she must feel so good without the horrid chemicals and constant attack on her. Even from here, I can see improvement. The humans are protecting themselves, and some of the crises of the viruses are being contained. Yes, it is time for another crisis.'

As the sun begins to rise and the morning brings a new light and life, Mother Nature descends to her private location deep within the Amazon forest, where the heart, soul, and Lungs of Mother Earth are protected.

"Morning, Mother Earth. How are you feeling?"

Mother Earth smiles, "Hello, my friend. Good morning to you, too. I am feeling great, I have to say my waters are cleaner, the air is so much fresher, even more than I have seen in a hundred Earth years. It feels so amazing. But it is hard not to hear the tears and anguish of the good souls suffering the wraith of the evil doers. The dark is affecting more than just the virus now; it is in the morality of the people. What a mess they have made of this. The cruel and unusual behaviors from some are difficult for me to continue to endure. It is getting dark all around me now; all my lands are infected now. What are you seeing from above she asked."

Mother Nature smiles, "You are right. The air and waters are already beginning to improve, but the humans are in the middle of a great division, which will determine the outcome for you, Mother Earth. Well, not so much you, because if it comes to it, the humans will be removed to protect you from complete destruction."

"I am getting so much love from the animals. They know what's up, but more improvements are needed right now. I did not know the extent of the evil growing in this world, and just how strong it has gotten. You'll see they are sacrificing each other even now, all for power and money again the downfall of society."

"If only they would see before it is too late. I am seeing some progress. At issue now is just how evil the corrupters are. The call of money is still too strong, and they are sacrificing the good people to continue raping the world for their personal benefit. We must convince the people to come together and to protect and save themselves. I find that most are still taking precautions, and those who are corrupted with greed are out in force. Those who created this immense hate cannot hide from this, as it is their creation and, therefore, it belongs to them. Your increased storms are showing the good that the greedy will only take from them; they will not help them. Yet I see the goodness and the kindness come through every single day; they are what give me great hope."

"Such hard times," says Mother Earth, "but I am feeling much stronger than ever. It's been a slow, painful death to me, but I am regaining faster than I expected, thank goodness. I am feeling a bit feisty lately, listening to the evil suggestions and plans that are being set up, so I am thinking of some major increases in the intensity and destruction of my storms. I am concerned about the suffering that is caused, but like you, I am witness to the kindness and generosity of humans. But I am asking for you to disrupt those abusing the lives of others. Those large disobedient crowds of hate that are minions of the evil, corrupt, and they are sacrificing themselves to kill others. I am begging you, Mother Nature, to assist me in a speedy removal of those individuals, for this will help us recover faster. I will not allow abuse to myself; I will not accept it anymore. Have you noticed the animals? She chuckles. They seem to be silly with excitement right now, but it feels so good. My concern is whether it will last."

Mother Nature smiles, "Yes, I have seen my animal kingdom so happy, and I admit it fills me up with happiness and strength. But we must not lose focus on the destructors who are intent on killing off the good people, so I must stay busy, and you too, as we are running out of time. Again, I call on all of my animals to come together and locate and destroy the evil and ill-minded that continue to roam the world. We need their help in order to succeed."

And with that, Mother Earth and Mother Nature continue the fight to protect the good and destroy the evil to the best of their abilities.

"So much work to do, but defeating this evil is what we will do." Exclaims Mother Nature as she retreats to her home upon Venus.

As the Earth days turn to months and then years, the World continues to fall into a whirlwind of chaos. Mother Nature and Mother Earth have been extraordinarily busy, but Mother Earth, it seems, is doing some amazing house cleaning, and the Earth is coming back with strength. Mother Nature descends again to the meadow deep in the heart of Mother Earth's core.

"Good day, Mother Earth. You appear to have been busy, my friend."

"Hello, Mother Nature. Yes, yes, I have. But let me tell you, I am not finished yet. First, I'm shaking it up some to bring the toxins to the surface, where I am ready with the super-powerful hurricanes and typhoons to get it off me and gone. Whew, let me tell you, while I am doing this, I am finding some truly foul humans set on destruction and cruelty that is too much for me to watch, so I decided to help with some clean up."

Mother Nature chuckles, "Yes, I have been watching, and what a job you have done. I feel a lot more hope from the humans now, but they are fighting a most horrid form of hate that I haven't seen on this soil for so long. I never thought it would be anything near that again, but I was wrong. The evil is certainly strong on Earth in a lot of ways. I even got a recent call from Luce, which was a very big surprise. He has also indicated his frustration and declared that this is in no way a path that he has any part in. In fact, I do believe he and The Almighty have been having some very interesting discussions regarding all that is transpiring."

"Really?" says Mother Earth, "Why? That is just...just, well, I don't know exactly what to say, Mother Nature. I have to say it's strange, but that gives me pause."

"I was surprised myself, but as I said to him, I appreciate the information and reaching out to me, like I said many times, we need to regroup ourselves and work together. But his world of hate and evil has no part on Earth, and if he wanted to help, he could. So he states he is tackling some of the darkest and most destructive happenings around the Earth, and I am eternally grateful for his assistance and expertise on handling this depth of evil. But I am not making a deal with the devil himself to fix an out-of-control member of his, that will be for him to contain and destroy."

"Wow," Mother Earth says, "you are not concerned about his deceit and lies?"

"No, Mother Earth, I am not. I, in a way, see a bit of what Luce was attempting to convey when he indicated man could not all be good. So, I myself never felt him as a partner or confidant, but he has shown us a different way that some humans could take evil to a level that goodness could not comprehend. It was too hard at that time to foresee such an evil on earth, and it is showing its depth right now. I admit he may have been correct, but he has opened the door for evil to grow. He is finding out now that he can be deceived as well.... Anyway, enough of him.

It is my concern now that those of us who oversee you will need to work together as one entity to save the humans that walk upon you."

Mother Earth, deep in thought, speaks out, "They have taken to torching me in the worst of times, Mother Nature, for my forest of cover is burning out of control as the humans fight to protect me, and they are losing. I give them all I have, and no matter what, they still stand up and fight for me. They have great moments of triumph, but they do not sustain.

Those are the ones we must watch over my friend, for the cruelty to mankind and to myself is something I haven't seen for so long and had hoped I never would, yet it is even worse than those dark evil times. Especially since mankind allowed it to return. I fear we are too late again."

"I hear you, my friend, and I will forever protect you and my children of nature, for they are suffering so much and their cries are so painful that I fear myself sometimes, but I must continue for my babies that are still in need. I do not understand these humans. I travel across the most beautiful lands you have upon you, glorious colors, deep waters, you are so majestic."

"We will prevail, my friend, but the fate of the humans is not mine to oversee, and I am always available to the Almighty if needed, as he watches the actions of our earthbound humans. Love is powerful, as you know. It is transforming, and we'll be better as soon as we all work together as we should, and those who cannot should no longer be allowed on this beautiful planet. They forget that it is a temporary visit, this crazy notion of what they call money does nothing in the next steps of a soul's journey, and I will leave it at that."

"I see, mother and father Redwood in our ancient forests have survived our recent fires; I fear for them. I have seedlings planted upon my lands at home, and I am blessed with their beautiful canopy. But the most distrustful and disturbing human activity is the demise of the Amazon rainforest. This forces the weather disturbance, and those changes will not relent, for the humans themselves must stop these actions, or their fate and the natural chain of life will be forever removed from your soils. This, I promise you, is the truth, and now my greatest fear."

With a sigh of fatigue and despair that seems to go on and on, Mother Earth softly replies, "Ah, my friend. These are such sad and sorrowful times; how painful this is to me and mankind."

"But I see goodness still, and I, and the humans, are helping to cure my ailments and mend my forest; they are in need of more help, so like you, I will continue to fight against evil destruction and protect the goodness that walks my soil."

"Did you see Mother Whale?"

"Yes, she has another child, and this test will mark the conservative work the humans are producing. I fear the cleanup is far from complete, but my hope is high for this little one."

"Isn't the baby beautiful?" grinned Mother Nature. "I will say again how proud I am of her, for she cried out to the entire planet as a final warning. I am grateful for her strength in such a painful time, she has made a tremendous change in the planet and has a beautiful new life to continue her legacy. Let us hope the humans continue to progress and not fall into the same routines as before."

"There is a dark evil growing rapidly and hovering over the lands of America. There is a danger of a level of evil and destruction spreading across the land and over the seas. Where is this power coming from? It is an enemy to the human race, and it is set on destroying you. This, my friend, is what we must focus on. The lies and secrets are coming out for you to see, and now is the time to lift the cover. Seek out the truths and add our findings to the goodness that is fighting against this. It is now time for our combined powers to engulf and uplift those who fight so hard to protect us. They are the keepers of the earth, and they need our powers. So, I again send the power of conviction and courage to the fighters on your soil, and together with you, we will all stand together and defeat this horrid darkness and proceed to a more promising future for all."

Mother Earth proudly declares her agreement, and as they wrap up their conversation and return to begin the plans they've created for positive change that they have in store for the humans on Mother Earth.

Days have turned into weeks, and the Earth is currently in a massive battle with another version of the virus set on death to humans. The cries and pain from the Earth are echoing throughout the stars and galaxies, yet the cruelty could have been so much less. Mother Earth is still in dire turmoil. She is becoming desperate to save herself at this time as the darkest of humans refuse to acknowledge that they are the main source of the death of her and the animals. Mother Nature's plans are heading back to earth for another attempt at instilling in humans the need for the entire circle of life's existence for humans to continue. She ponders how, after all this time, the human race has not understood the basic knowledge of the circle of life, their position in the chain, and the finality if this chain is forever severed.

As Mother Nature arrives, her heart feels the heaviness of complete sadness and despair.

"Mother Earth," she says, "how are you, my friend?"

Mother Earth sighs, "I feel the defeat in the depths of my core, my friend. The goodness is getting conquered by the evil and selfishness of so many humans, more than I would have thought. How did we not see this, I wonder. They just do not care! They have destroyed their moral compasses. They even refuse to believe, and I cannot believe in them anymore. I must find the poison that has possessed so many. They do not understand or believe that I can stop this? It will cost the humans' lives, but will save the animals and the Earth. My storms are growing greater than ever before. I'm using all my elements, but I am faced with the strongest evil resistance. It's as if they themselves are destroying humans for domination. I have not seen such evil in a long time, and like before, it will not succeed. Mother Nature. I cannot tell you how this has saddened me. I feel it may be best to wipe them off the planet now, or I may not make it myself. It sounds so final. My storms will produce levels never seen before. This illness shall be directed and increased on the evil and destructive souls on my soil."

"But it is not hurting the humans it should. Where is their protection coming from?"

"Are you sure that Luce has nothing to do with this rush of evil and deceit? It feels like that kind of evil to me."

Mother Nature replies, "I understand, my friend, so many are trying so hard to stop the spread of this evil, and we must do what we can to increase their strengths and propel them to the positions across the lands that will position them to conquer those most destructive selfish entities that are poisoning you. There are signs of hope from the humans, but I agree they are not fully engaging in this fight of good and evil. It is so much more, I am set to display for the world and point out individually those that are the worst, and that my friend, will become the list of who is no longer permitted on your soil. The Almighty has been very patient with this group, but our eyes are open to the fact that a good majority lost, or we could say sold their soul and expected to be the ones to defeat all that is good. Those are the humans that shall no longer prevail. We can do this, my friend. All of us are working together, but we must stay strong and stay as one."

"Remember also that this will take time. It came to be over a long period on your soil, and it will take the same amount to evict it from your soil and the Cosmos above. These souls will never proceed in growth; they will die and be no more."

Mother Earth sighs, "Yes, I know, and I am with you. It's just so hard for me to see the goodness anymore, for I am exhausted myself, and at times I feel despair. I must rest now, as always, it is uplifting to talk with you. Enjoy my lands before you head home."

Mother Nature smiles and waves as she wanders to her favorite places to spend some time with her beloved creatures. Reassuring them that she is and will always protect them.

Days have turned to weeks now and into years. Mother Nature and Mother Earth have been hard at work together with the Almighty, and all that oversees the humans and our cosmos, are now together discussing with a collective sadness the excessive clouds of Evil followers that have been unleashed in numbers they cannot believe but now see for themselves. So much sadness and despair from the humans is felt throughout. Mother Nature excuses herself to ascend for a visit with Earth to update her.

Mother Nature softly speaks, "Are you doing alright, Mother Earth? The viruses and this evil have exhausted our humanity; most of the good are fighting to save or fighting to live. Sadly, many good souls are present at the gates of heaven, overwhelming the humans and destroying their spirits. This is affecting our fight. I understand your anger and pain. These storms are difficult to contain. The changes in your core are fueling the powerful winds and rains that I'm losing so many of our beautiful creatures that I've sent to help you thrive. Is there anything that can be done to decrease the intensity as we direct our fight to evil that is set on the complete destruction of you?"

Mother Earth sighs in a feeling of defeat. "My friends, as you know, a lot of this is no longer in any of our control. We are at a point with the humans where they must come together, or as you're all observing, I will no longer be able to keep them here, or should I say, want them here. I am doing all I can to protect those of good heart, but like you, I find that evil spreads very rapidly even after the containment of the virus, almost as if they were one and the same. Was this virus a guise for this evil, I wonder. But for you, I will do my best. I can feel all the help you and the others are doing. My hope is that more humans come together and join our fight. Thank you for your support and for my visit. I do look forward to our talks. See you again soon, my friend, and say hello to the others for me."

More and more time has elapsed on Mother Earth, and the fury of storms and destructive disasters is also pointing out the horrid corruption and greed that have plagued humans continuously. It has now begun to show those behind the evil deeds exactly as we were hoping. Mother Earth has instructed the elements and literally frozen the ground to places not seen in hundreds of years, and sadly, more have suffered amidst this fight, but also more are finally realizing the world around them is being destroyed. More humans are teaming up together as we hoped, yet we need so many more. Still, there is hope for all.

Mother Nature has focused attention on critical areas that are causing Mother Earth to react so aggressively, and the animals are working together responding to the crisis as a group, regardless of species. Sadly, this is how humans normally react. Yet, this time it is savagely different. So much selfishness and greed, Mother Nature thought sadly, still, the light of love is showing, and the need for help is growing stronger. The Almighty has a plan she knows, but it's the road to achievement that is the toughest. The need for frivolous things must stop dominating their minds, or humankind will cease to exist due to suicide by greed. Heavily saddened, Mother Nature spreads her light beyond, showering the goodness in souls with strength and comfort as they continue the fight for kindness and civility amongst an evil set to destroy whomever it chooses. "Stay strong, my friends," she whispers through the wind.

"When needed, look to nature and animals, for they see and feel your pain and will bring you peace and strength. Be strong, my friends, and share your sadness with us, for we can assist in bringing you comfort. Sit quietly in the forest, the seas, the meadows, and see. You can hear nature if you just listen. Staring down upon the earth, she is hopeful they hear her words."

There is again a beautiful golden glow approaching Mother Nature's balcony. "Oh, lovely," she thought. "The Almighty is here for a visit."

"Hello, my friend. How are you doing?" The Almighty says as the light settles upon her balcony.

Mother Nature gently speaks. "Hello to you, my friend, I am charged with hope and love. I hear your worries within my thoughts and wish to thank you for all you are doing. The pain upon the earth is severe, and your help at this time is greatly appreciated by us all."

The Almighty nodding in agreement, "It is a tough time, but fear not, we have weathered horrible times before, and we will again. How this crisis is approached and received is what will determine the direction or current course on Mother Earth, but for now, we must help where we can and watch and see how the humans react together. It is hard to see those who choose against, but that is the choice in their heart and not of concern to us. They choose to deny, they lose our guidance and grace, which is important for me to convey. Humans all have choices, and only they can determine what they choose to do with their time on Earth. There is more goodness and kindness than we see; some are hiding in fear, and some are quietly making a difference all over the land. I bless all those souls with confidence and good fortune to prepare them for their journey. Mother Nature, I must tell you I have called back the angels that oversee our beloved humans who have decided on hate, individualism, and immense cruelties. My simple request of love and kindness to all is quite a simple deed, and at this time, I no longer stand for those who cross the line of love and truly hate. As I said before, it is their choice to make, as it is my choice on the ramifications of those choices. This I am sharing with you so you may prepare yourself for an increase in the cries from those who cry in vain, and to disassociate yourself from their pains, as they are not for anything but themselves, and they cry out the loudest. There are many throughout the lands of Earth that are standing up to the evil, and it is those humans that I envelop with my light and love."

Mother Nature, listening intently to his words, answers, "I understand and completely agree with your wisdom, and I appreciate you coming to visit and share your thoughts and decisions. May I ask how you are doing?"

Softly and with a bright, radiant glow, He says, "I am doing well, and it warms a soul when another expresses such a kindness, and I thank you, and again, yes, I am doing well, but continue absorbing as much pain and sadness as possible. With that said, I do need to take myself back home, but I couldn't pass up a chance to sit with you on your balcony in your glorious home. I want to thank you again, Mother Nature, for all you do and are doing."

"You're welcome, of course, and I love your visits even for a short time. Call on me anytime, and as you know, I will be there."

With that, he recedes away, and Mother Nature is set to start another day, digesting the words the Almighty has said. "I must keep going," she says to herself. "Always so much to do."

Another fragment of Earth time has passed, and the crisis is now hitting critical levels. Mother Earth is in critical condition at this point in time, and Mother Nature sadly gazes down upon her. "What more can we do she says, deep in thought, so many human souls are suffering. They need our strengths and more Almighty. I know you said to let it happen, but as you know, it is painful to see. I must do something. With what I can, I shall insert even more strength within and increased foresight along with unblocked pathways to succeed in our mutual goal of defeating the evil and destructive behaviors which have affected Mother Earth. With this extreme power sent, it will destroy the evil upon her soil. I grant this to all those who are worthy of such power, knowing that above all, it can never be used in an evil form against goodness; it will die first. I send this to them in seeds of hope and good fortune. It is and will always be for the protection of Mother Earth, the animal kingdom, and our beloved Universe. I am here, my children, I am working, and I am watching."

Earth months have passed. Mother Earth's health is still quite critical, and the fury of all that is transpiring is doing irreparable damage to her core. "How can all this be happening?" she ponders. "How are so many humans not angry and fighting to save this world? Why are they letting it all die?"

"She has all hands on deck within the nature world upon Mother Earth, and they are also losing this battle of good and evil that's playing out upon the lands. The numbers lost in these elemental storms are more than anyone could have predicted, and more are being lost. Oh, how I wish the humans could hear our cries, open their minds, and set out to protect her. Why are they hiding!"

Mother Nature descends again upon her special spot overlooking the beautiful lands of Earth in all its wonder. "Hello, my friend. I sit here and just stare at the beauty of the land. So remarkably beautiful, the colors and the smells are rich with life. How there can still be so much hate and destruction is just something I will never understand, and I am so sorry for all the pain and suffering you're still experiencing. I hear through your winds those snippets of hope, but still, there is much to be concerned about."

"I will not lose hope for this kingdom. No matter what may happen, your lands will always be returned to this beautiful state. Humans may ruin their chances to be here, but you, my friend, will never die. I am going to walk upon you and see all I can of my creatures and reassure them also of my love and protection. Then back home I shall go. I will come back to you again soon."

The spawn of Evil upon the Earth has awoken. Returning Mother Nature sits again upon her favorite spot to speak with Mother Earth. "My friend, it is time, as you can feel the evil and its destructive weapons are crashing upon you with disregard for any forms of life. The toxic weapon of power is being wielded before the world as if using it would accomplish anything other than complete annihilation of all who reside here."

"What is the driving force of this evil, I wonder. What is the endgame for you? There is a new evil upon you; it is greater than all before it. It can poison a human brain and soul without their knowledge. We must find its source before time for humans runs out."

Mother Earth gently speaks, "My friend, I feel it is happening now. The people have a true courageous leader, finally, who is standing up to evil with nothing but honor to defend it. But this cannot be done by one; it will take many. My ground is rumbling with bombs and fire, but it is also filled with love, togetherness, and a sense of unity I have never seen before. I can feel the power of the good, and it is getting stronger every minute. You've directed the animal kingdom to fight, and they are succeeding, and the humans are gathering, all over the world. We must assist them if we can increase the strength of my storms and the strength of my quakes. We must protect my core. Our beautiful Amazon forest is nearly destroyed, and where you sit now is all that is left of my lungs. The humans never understood that you placed so many deterrents here for a reason. Poison frogs and insects and more were placed for my protection. So many protective animals, but they are destroyed when the machines kill the land. Soon, I will not be able to control the storms, temperatures, and quakes. More souls will be lost if not all that is. Earth time for life as we are witnessing is at its breaking point, and all the goodness within the humans must come together, as I am tired."

From the skies above, the Almighty watches and listens to Mother Earth's pleas and all that is transpiring. "It is so troubling, and he is concerned for all as he sees ahead an even greater evil disaster that is about to engulf the world. Collecting his angels and the powers within, he begins to prepare for what's to come. Where is this evil coming from? He knows but is unable to do the work for the humans; they must do it themselves."

Time goes by, and the world is driven deeper into despair. Evil is present on multiple lands, and bombs are again dropping and killing the innocent and good. Fight is all we can do, but the weapons are beyond evil comprehension. Mother Earth calls out, "They are poisoning me faster now, my veins, my water, and my land. The blood of the good rains into my soil from evil, what we all thought would never happen again, but it is."

Mother Earth calls up to Mother Nature with such sadness in her soul. "My friend, I need your help. We are all dying, and they are destroying the sources that give life to our circle of life. The chain is breaking, the human morals are being destroyed, and death is happening all over my lands. Death of goodness, kindness, and all things which make me thrive. I'm begging you, my friend and the Almighty, to allow powers of goodness to fall upon those fighting to protect me and each other. We need more assistance as the evil has no rules, and comprehending the depths of this cruelty is something too awful to comprehend. It is time to help them! They fear taking themselves to the level of evil needed to defeat this monster, so I, Mother Earth, am begging the powers above to step in and assist. Give them the power of Knowledge to see the path to defeat, the courage to stand up to the monster without fear, and the protection to do this and succeed. It is time. It has started by destroying a country by force, then another, and all with lies and evil machines, but it is only the beginning. Evil is awake in every part of my lands, and I need it revealed and destroyed. I have my own weapon of mass destruction, which, if I choose to use, will end all life on me for thousands of years or forever. I fear that if I do not completely destroy myself, the evil I have witnessed will return. It will be crueler than before. I may use my weapon to destroy myself and all that I am forever. I will implode myself to no longer be in existence. That is how tired I am of this. So again, I call out to the powers above to stop this before it is too late, for I fear it is about to become irreversible for all."

Mother Nature, in her home, listens to Mother Earth's words rising up to the heavens as she begs for help, and she, too, is at a loss. The evil has interfered in her positions, altering viruses, altering the minds of my animals to be used for evil; all the boundaries that have stood throughout time are now crossed. She calls out to the Almighty, asking "at what point can we step in, when our boundaries are destroyed, should we not enlist our armies to descend and enforce that which has so cruelly defied us? All we know and all we have protected is in peril, and I believe it is now up to us to enrich the goodness standing with us all the things Mother Earth has asked for. The rules have been broken, and it is up to us to assist them in defeating this horrid rush of evil. I, too, am now begging for us to give love, life, strength, knowledge, and courage to succeed in the world war, so I, too, call on all of us to come together, for you are the Almighty, and the suffering is growing rapidly, and we must use all our powers to succeed. It is Time. With all that I am, I myself send to evil the pain and suffering of mental illnesses, cancers, and viruses to enter the bodies of evil and invade the brains and hearts rapidly, so that they cannot be treated. No more will evil doers be immune to the pains and destruction of these weapons of evil. I send them directly to the decision makers hiding behind walls and ordering the death of goodness with a falsehood. This I say with all my might and implement around the world at lightning speed to any unsavable souls that boldly defy the natural order of life, no more. From right this moment, a cruel and painful end to those lives starts now. Upon those words, I declare it now."

Her frustration showing and aware she is crossing the boundaries she knows not to cross, her anger so intense, she knows she must calm herself to think rationally of a possible solution for Earth and her precious animal kingdom.

Sitting on her balcony that overlooks those precious animals that have been removed from the surface of Earth to come here to either evolve and return or upgrade to the next dimension. Her heart is heavy still. The beauty of these creatures fills her heart and calms her spirit. She gains her patience and waits.

It has now been what Earth counts as four months, and the turmoil is at its highest levels of all time. Mother Earth is involved in her biggest battle with evil as it continues to deplete her resources and destroy her soul, all for the greed of a few and the cost of the lives of many. She is patient; her faith in the goodness of many will prevail; she believes that completely.

She is aware of a presence coming to her, and moments later, the Almighty appears upon her balcony, also with noted sadness to his presence. Knowing he also heard her words and the cries of Earth.

"Hello, Mother Nature. I have come to see you myself out of concern for your well-being after your last venture to Mother Earth. How are you feeling?"

"Hello to you," she says, "I am deeply grateful for your visit today. Although I must say you yourself radiate similar stresses as I, so much anguish. I have been reflecting and watching over our friend, Mother Earth, and I am not seeing a swing in her defenses or much protection from the humans placed upon her. And now one of my personal nature protectors and confidant of earth has been called to your heavens, leaving behind a worldwide hole upon the lands and the good givers."

"How is Jane? She is greatly missed by many; the children she so believed in are coming together from every corner of the world. She accomplished so much in her time, but still, it is a deep loss for the Earth."

"Aw, yes." The almighty sighs, "It was time for her to rise, and the services given by her were pure and honest. I have a great need for her, yet I agree it was a great loss for the land, but as you are aware, there are many who also have those skills and passions. She taught many with her beliefs and knowledge. Let us see who steps up and continues her work. Were it not for the savage greed in which Mother Earth is enduring. We would be so much more advanced. It is painful to observe the mass amounts of evil continuing by spreading across all the lands, but we must not slow in our efforts to support goodness with all we can do without the interference of free will."

With a sigh, Mother Nature looks to the Almighty and says, "I understand why we cannot interfere, but I also believe that the evil is being fueled within by Luce himself, and he is seeming to be succeeding in his goals. Is that not also a form of forced free will, giving humans momentum with material things and phony forms of success with what they call money?"

"I understand," the Almighty says, "but as hard as it is to comprehend, they are choices made by the humans themselves. They are choosing to follow falsehoods and praise a God who is not a part of the Cosmos or follows any of my teachings, and those individuals will burn for the cruelties they are producing. It is unfortunate that the number of followers of the lies and greed upon the Earth is growing in numbers, but again, this is a choice they are making. Just remember that evil lives by smoke and mirrors. Meaning they may not be as strong or as many as they appear. We can all be easily fooled by that."

"Mother Earth is increasing her surface destruction, and there is not one element she has that humans can overcome. They will either come together to support each other, or they will be destroyed, and then they face the creators for the review of their lives; that is when consequences shall be placed upon them. What you and I can do meanwhile is support those souls upon the Earth who are there standing for kindness, goodness, compassion, and Unity. What Luce is doing is to beat down and rejoice in any defeat; that is what angers me, and that is where we need to focus. Mother Earth is powerful enough to destroy all of mankind and can handle the evils in her own way. We must remember that it is the humans of goodness, as I've said, that we must support and guide."

Sighing but in agreement with the Almighty's words, Mother Nature smiles. "Yes, you are right, of course, and I thank you for reminding me of these points. It must be just as difficult for you to witness the demise of mankind as it is for me to witness the demise of the lovely animal kingdom."

"I will do as you suggest and continue the fight. Thank you again for coming, it is always welcome and calming."

EARTHYEAR 2026

In what seems like the blink of an eye to Mother Nature, years have passed, and the fight for goodness continues upon the Earth, and sadly, a very large surge of evil and lies has again prevailed in the lands of the Americas. "It is as I have feared," Mother Nature thinks. She is gazing beyond her home upon the planet Venus towards the beautiful Earth and her beloved kingdom of animals. Sadly, she bears witness to Mother Earth, who, with all her might, warned the humans of what their treacherous drillings, bombs, sonars, and chemicals were doing to her; she has now had enough.

"She needs me," Mother Nature feels and is preparing herself for a descent onto the Earth's lands to visit and stand with her beloved friend. But first, she thinks a request for a visit with the Almighty is something she must do first. They each have changes and decisions that must be made now. Human destruction is in need of a decisive halt, and how and when is on the table for discussion now.

As she sits and prepares for her guest, she reflects on the achievements of these last few years. 'Progress had been made, and the fight against the injustices was continuing with noticeable forms of cheating that, for some reason, became the norm, and when all was on the table for a positive shift for all, A seemingly vast majority of humans chose the path on which they were about to embark. A path so desolate and broken, they will most likely not prevail, and that is now in motion, and we are unable to stop. Oh, how desperate we were for the kindness and light to blow out the dark and set up this planet for years and years. But we, as those upon the earth, watched with heavy hearts as evil, greed, cruelty, and hate filled the senses and destroyed everything we have worked so hard to protect.' Mother Nature sighs a heavy sigh, but with that breath, she also solidifies her desire to protect her children on Earth and the souls dedicated to them and Earth. 'It is time,' she thinks, 'for me to step up my involvement and directly take some actions. I shall start with fundamental powers for my animal humans who care for my kingdom every day, either by saving or protecting them and their environment, or caring for the ill or injured. They shall have the ability to hear and understand my animal kingdom, to use that knowledge as they work to protect them now. They will save the world from evil using a gift only known to them. I give them insight, knowledge, wisdom, patience, and luck. Lol, yes, luck she thinks, we can all use that.'

Just then, as the air began to change, Mother Nature was aware of her guest's arrival. Chuckling, the Almighty says to her, "My dear, that is quite a declaration you have chosen. However, I do agree with your intent, and I, too, shall express my desire for increasing the abilities of our souls, which prevail against so much adversary. The luck part is key, of course, lol."

"Hello, my friend," she smiles, "It is always such a good moment when we get a chance to just spend a bit of time together. Thank you for coming."

"How are you doing yourself, Mother Nature? I was saddened to see the death of our newest baby Orca whale again after all this time. Such a statement to all regarding the destruction of Earth. But as you have said many times, the humans are not paying any attention. Maybe your gift of insight will help the helpers; we shall see."

"I am planning a visit to. Mother Earth, she is definitely done waiting, and I cannot blame her. My faith in the majority of Earth is still intact, but we must continue to assist with some form of slowdown of the momentum this evil has taken."

"Mother Earth is doing everything within her power. I will not deny her the right to save herself from the destruction of mankind that walks upon her on borrowed time. So I do agree with your application of insight to those worthy of the gift, I will still withhold my sword and temptation to interfere, as I still have hope and belief that goodness will prevail and win in the long term. Is it hard to witness such atrocities? Yes, it is in my name that they apply their hate! Something that will mark their soul for eternity. As hard as it is to watch Mother Nature, I do have the final determination of the soul in my possession. Mine are not rules; they are goals. You must achieve these life goals fully and completely in order to advance. There is no cheat way to proceed; however, if a man decides to repeat this knowledge in books, bibles, writings, etc., it is fine, but each soul is very aware of these written or embedded goals. It is in their DNA. It's the key to the Earth world. Without the key to each level of knowledge, you cannot advance. It is so simple, yet they cloud their own heads with foolishness and lies. Why would I make the life lessons hard? That's for later chapters," he adds with a twinkling wink.

HE shifts his glance to Mother Nature and speaks these words firmly. "I stand with you today with your suggestion to apply your ability of insight to the worthy workers on the land. I, too, shall apply the cloak of knowledge, insight, and wisdom along with yours to equal the disadvantage being used against the good and honorable. This cloak shall divert the extreme hate and cruelty of the days to come, shall form a protection of the soul to never be devoured by the hate and evil before it, unless it is by their choice, and finally, the cloak of love and protection to the heart and soul of the humans it is protecting. Yes, we shall start with that and monitor with my best angels to assist as needed. Let's start there, Mother Nature."

"I agree," she nods. "And might I say that it goes very well with my words."

She chuckles softly, "I love your insights; they are very thought-out and straightforward. It always fills me with happiness and hope. Thank you. Now, let's see if we can bring out some of that hope and love on our Earth. It's going to be a hard fight again to witness, but this time, I believe we are much more prepared. I said it before; this will take the entire World to defeat. Not just one Country or Land can accomplish this task. I just wonder if it will be this Generation of souls that can accomplish it."

The Almighty smiles, and with an inner light that beams so beautifully. "It is always good to visit with you, my dear, but I must be off. Send my love and hellos to Mother Earth for me on your visit and let her know we are there for her needs, whatever they may be."

And then he was gone, almost as quickly as he came. Left alone again, Mother Nature sits quietly reflecting on the visit and making her plans to visit her dear friend Mother Earth.

It is January in the year 2026. Mother Earth has been fighting for her very life in the years leading up to now, but the level of disease she fights has reached a fever point. She is Angry. She is tired, and she is done with all the torment and destruction upon her soul.

"My inner core is not able to protect me much longer she feels. I must remove this toxic and destructive position that humans are presenting. I do not understand why they bother. Nuclear poison for whom? It does nothing but destroy me, me who provides everything for everyone that lives upon me. Evil greed that tortures my veins and poisons my water, killing all that I have nourished in all of my many years. Nothing, I think, has ever been as destructive and as disgusting as what is upon me in these current times, and I have seen it all."

"I am done. I am angry, yes, I am calling upon my elements of Fire! Ice! Wind! Rains and the fissures of my core to expand... With all I have in me, I shall prevail, and mankind will not. This is the fault of the evils of man, the fault of continued greed for seeking a monetary possession that is meaningless in the scope of life. Such a waste to the souls that walk upon me that have done so very much to protect. My release is not to harm you, as I know that you'll band together in my angry release and protect each other, care for each other, and me while I continue to ravage myself with destruction to show all who doubt that I am ready. I am ready to remove mankind. I am ready for the ignorant bombs that small-minded men tout as meaningful. I will remove it all."

Just then, through the glittering sky above and into the most beautiful meadow of all, Mother Nature ascends to her favorite rock perch again. Overlooking the absolute beauty in front and all around her.

Mother Earth, says Mother Nature with sparkling eyes, "This is just so pretty, so unbelievably beautiful. Every time I get a chance to visit my children, there is an awe-inspiring beauty to your lands. Wow."

"How are you? She asks. Has there been any improvement to your core? I can see you're very frustrated with the changes again coming against you, and I've come to just listen."

"Ahhh, hello," says Mother Earth. "Yes, I do love it when you come to see the home you trust for your children. The animals, the plants, the insects, the beautiful chain of life are all a part of your beautiful world that helps fulfil mine. Always takes a team to make something the best, that's what I say."

"Seriously, though, I am not well. I hurt, and I am sick. I am glad you've come down because I need you to understand the steps I must take in order to protect myself. I fear for your animal kingdom, and the Almighty's mankind kingdom will suffer much as I purge the vile devices and poisons which have been and are being used against and inside me. I am heating the freeze and freezing the heat. I am burning the lush land and soaking the desert, I am splitting my core to extract and reject that which has been used upon and against me. I am done."

Mother Nature sat quietly, listening to her old friend, and sadly, she understands what needs to be done.

"The Almighty and I have granted some distinct powers and foresight to those who are worthy enough to understand and use the skills that should be of some assistance to you. The Almighty has also laid upon the lands the thousands of angelic souls needed for protection upon your soils as these changes come into being. We understand and accept what you must do and will be right there working for solutions every step of the way. You will be saved, my friend. We will lose good souls in order to achieve it, but it must be done. My animal kingdom is at your side. We have many powers to out the evil which is upon us, and as of today and forward, the world will continue to see things they have never seen or experienced before. This will not end until the evil is destroyed and our world is realigned in the powers of goodness, kindness, and above all, honesty."

With a heavy sigh and a heavy heart, Mother Nature proceeds down across the meadow to a place where she will notify the animal kingdom of what is to come and how they will help. As for mankind, well, we have to see if the powers granted are enough to help elevate the hard work those of true heart have done, and if they will defeat the evil upon earth before earth defeats the evil itself. Countdown is on.

"I'm heading home again. Stand strong, my friend, and we shall talk again soon."

In her heart, she is filled with the hope that the goodness in mankind will come together and stand as one against the evils that are attacking them and the Earth they reside on.

"Can they do it? Will they do it?"

Her thoughts returned to Luce. 'He is using his skills to enrage the humans to fight each other. He has always wanted that, proof that he was right. He never once took himself out of the fight. And now he again presents the illusion of winning a human experiment of good and evil that, if he succeeds, is not a win at all. That's what he does.'

Humans have always believed that there is more goodness and that it will always prevail. But Luce has always promoted falsehoods, and they are chosen by so many who are being fooled.

To mankind I say, "let us all stand upon the lands of Mother Earth and check in with her. She needs us to step up. She really, truly needs the humans to save her."

As the Almighty watches Mother Nature return home, her thoughts ring out, listening, he hears her keeping up the hope and sharing again the love and thankfulness for what Mother Earth is and has been enduring in protecting as many of her beloved animals and the souls on the land as possible.

Mankind is at the point where decisions and choices need to be made. Time on Earth is running out, for if evil prevails, the Earth will not.

We wait......